THAILAND

THE GOLDEN KINGDOM

Dear Exotic Enchantment Winner,

We're glad you could join us in Thailand.
Thanks to your exceptional achievement,
our adventure has been a great success!

Photography by Luca Invernizzi Tettoni

Text by William Warren

 ASIA BOOKS

Published and distributed in Thailand by
Asia Books Co., Ltd.
5 Sukhumvit Road, Soi 61,
P.O. Box 40
Bangkok 10110, Thailand
Tel: (662) 714-0740-2, ext. 221-223
Fax: (662) 381-1621, 391-2277

Publisher : Eric Oey
Editor : Kim Inglis
Production : Violet Wong

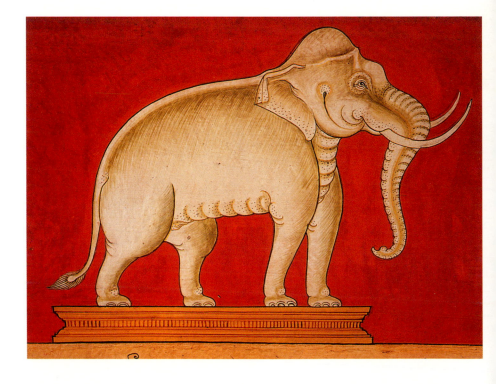

Right: The sacred white elephant, once a symbol of Thailand.
Opposite: The spires of the Temple of the Emerald Buddha, within the compound of the Grand Palace.

CONTENTS

"I do not know that these Siamese *wats* have beauty, which they say is reserved and aloof and very refined, all I know is that they are strange and gay and odd, their lines are infinitely distinguished, like the lines of a proposition in a schoolboy's Euclid, their colors are flaunting and crude, like the colors of vegetables in the greengrocer's stall at an open-air market, and, like a place where seven ways meet, they open roads down which the imagination can make many a careless and unexpected journey."

— Somerset Maugham, *The Gentleman in the Parlor* (1930)

INTRODUCTION

Among Thailand's traditional crafts, one of the most striking is mosaics made of glass or ceramic—intricate patterns created by fitting thousands of small pieces together into what looks from a distance like a solid mass of vivid color, only revealing its separate parts at closer inspection. You can see this art brought to a peak of perfection in the dazzling precincts of the Temple of the Emerald Buddha in the Grand Palace or at the famous Temple of Dawn which raises its porcelain encrusted towers over the Chao Phraya River.

The technique may also be used as a metaphor for Thailand itself. For the kingdom, too, is made up of many different components, so closely connected it takes time and not a little effort to appreciate them individually.

Bangkok, the point of entry for most visitors, is a prime example. At first glance the capital city seems a typical modern metropolis—vast (sprawling over 960 square km), overcrowded (with a population of at least twelve million, probably more), boasting a network of elevated expressways and an international skyline of highrise office towers, hotels and shopping centers.

But look a little more carefully, not far behind this familiar Western facade, and you discover another, quite different

Previous page, left: Gold elephant dating from the 15th century, found in one of the old temples of Ayutthaya.
Previous page, right: The ruins of Sukhothai, the first capital of Thailand, founded in the early 13th century.
Left: The Grand Palace compound; the golden spires are part of the Temple of the Emerald Buddha.
Right: His Majesty King Bhumibol Adulyadej on his throne in the Grand Palace, beneath the royal umbrella.

Thais are not the only people who have chosen to make their home in this land of fertile rice fields, misty mountains and sunny sea coasts. There are sizeable communities of ethnic Lao, Chinese, Cambodians, Malays and Mons, as well as semi-nomadic tribal groups in the north–all of whom regard Thailand as home and all of whom have contributed in some way to its distinctive culture.

There are imposing ruins of ancient capitals and monuments– not only Thai but also Khmer and Mon–going back nearly 1,000 years, as well as much older traces of prehistoric cultures. There is scenery of immense beauty (over 90 areas are national parks or wildlife preserves), and villages where traditional crafts and lifestyles have been only lightly touched by the modern world. At the same time, there are booming provincial capitals with all the amenities (and problems) of fabled Bangkok, internationally famous resorts and swift means of modern communication.

Thailand's revered monarchy has managed to adapt itself to demands of the contemporary world without losing its rich traditions and ceremonial grandeur. Also still vigorously alive are other memorable parts of the old cultural fabric: enduring faiths (Buddhism most prominently, but others as well); an internationally celebrated cuisine; sports (try an evening at Thai boxing to discover how different that is); and an almost endless array of festivals, rituals and classic arts found nowhere else.

"Amazing" is the word selected by the Tourism Authority of Thailand to sum up this diverse land. And amazing it most certainly is–full of beauty both natural and man-made, full of serendipitous surprises. It is a country that constantly draws its visitors back to discover yet another part of its complex pattern.

city: It is one that encompasses Buddhist temples at once serene and spectacular; picturesque canals lined with open-fronted houses; colorful markets piled with exotic products; a Chinatown of narrow, clamorous alleyways; old Victorian palaces set in lush gardens; and a great river teeming with timeless traffic.

Elsewhere, too, there is a similar co-existence of old and new, of cultural and scenic contrasts. Thailand is known as the "Land of the Free"; except for brief interludes in the 16th and 18th centuries, when the Burmese occupied the capital and other areas, it has always been proudly independent, undisturbed by colonial conquest and enjoying a degree of social and political unity rare among the countries of Southeast Asia. Yet, again, a closer look reveals surprising diversity.

Left: In one of the many rituals associated with theatre in Thailand, two classical dancers pay homage to their teachers by lighting candles and incense sticks at a shrine.
Right: A young classical dancer; the elaborate jewelled costumes, inspired by court dress during the Ayutthaya period, are works of art in themselves.

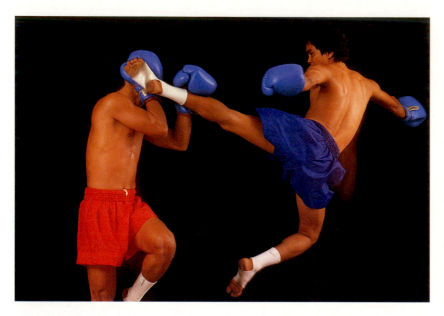

Aspects of Thai life. **Top, left:** Thai boxing, a sport that involves grace as well as ferocity. **Top, right:** Buddhist monks meditating in a field. **Bottom, left:** Elephants in the famous roundup held annually in Surin province. **Bottom, right:** Dancers in traditional costume.

Top, left: A procession carrying lustral water during the northern Songkran festival. **Top, right:** Members of the Royal Guard taking part in the Trooping of the Colors in Bangkok. **Bottom, left:** Students learning the classical dance gestures. **Bottom, right:** Members of the Akha hilltribe gather for a festival.

"When the Waters begin to retreat, the People return them Thanks for several Nights altogether with a great Illumination, not only for that they are retired, but for the Fertility which they render to the Lands. The whole River is then seen covered with floating Lanterns which pass with it... Moreover, to thank the Earth for its Harvest they do on the first days of their Year make another magnificent Illumination..."

— Simon de la Loubere, *A New Historical Relation of the Kingdom of Siam* (1691)

HISTORY

The earliest inhabitants of what is today Thailand are known only in shadowy form, through the assorted tools and ornaments they created. Some of these have been found in Kanchanaburi Province, along the River Kwai, others elsewhere in the country. The most dramatic discoveries came in a tiny hamlet called Ban Chiang in the northeast. Here, from around 3600 BC to 250 AD, an enigmatic people not only cultivated lowland rice but practised the art of bronze metallurgy, at a time much earlier than previously suspected. They also lived in houses, wove textiles, had domestic animals and fashioned objects that showed a refined sense of beauty.

The origin of these people remains a mystery. So does their fate, though some experts suggest they may have been the first of a series of migrant groups who were attracted to the fertile Chao Phraya valley and river basin. Two of the most important arrivals here were the Khmers and the Mons. Khmer culture reached its culmination in the splendors of Angkor, in the 12th century, but they also established cities deep in present-day Thailand. The Mons founded the Dvaravati Kingdom in the western half of the Chao Phraya valley and produced some of the earliest Buddhist monuments; their ancestors still live in the area.

The Thais, who would become the predominant group, are thought to have migrated from southern China into northern Thailand during the 11th century AD. By the 12th century, several independent Thai kingdoms had been established in the north, where they

formed a federation known as Lanna Thai. Some had penetrated down into territories theoretically controlled by Mons and Khmers. In 1238, two Thai chieftans joined together, overthrew a local Khmer commander and founded the kingdom of Sukhothai. Though it lasted only a little more than two centuries, Sukhothai was the scene of extraordinary development in art and culture, as well as in politics. Here the Thai alphabet was devised, and the first distinctly Thai forms of architecture and sculpture took shape; moreover, through a system of treaties and alliances, Thai power spread until it was felt over a considerably larger area than the country occupies today.

Ayutthaya, which ruled for four centuries, was a more complex kingdom, one that demonstrated to an even greater degree the Thai gift for assimilation. At its peak, in the 17th century, the capital was larger than London of the same period and as cosmopolitan. Besides the Khmers, Mons, Lao and Burmese with whom the Thais had co-existed for centuries, traders came from India, China, Japan and distant Persia. The first Europeans also arrived, and soon there were Dutch, English, Portuguese, and French "factories," or trading posts, doing business outside the walls of the city.

Previous page, left: The gold handle of a sword that forms part of the Royal Regalia.
Previous page, right: Painting in the throne hall of the Chakri Maha Prasat, showing Sir John Bowring being received in audience by King Rama IV in 1855.
Left: The remains of Sukhothai and **(right)** Ayutthaya. Both these ancient capitals were laid out according to ancient Hindu cosmological patterns, with the sacred Mount Meru as the center. This was also followed at Angkor. Dominating the view of Ayutthaya is Wat Phra Ram, modelled on Khmer architectural style.

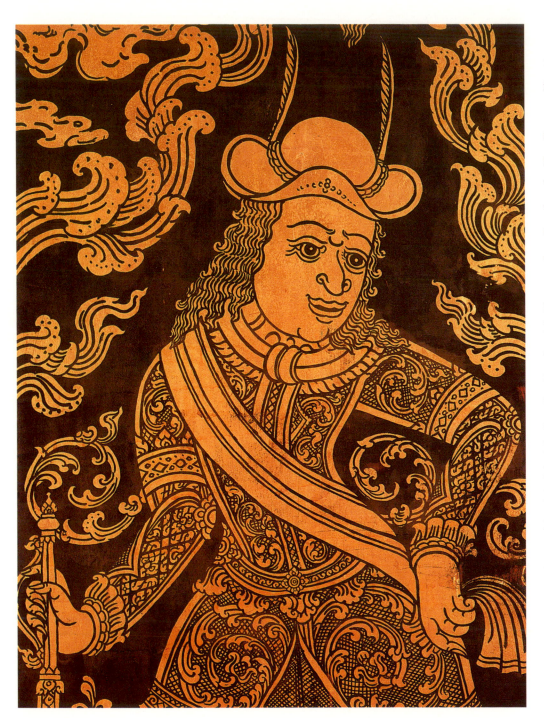

Following the destruction of Ayutthaya by the Burmese in 1767, the capital was moved further south, first to Dhonburi and finally to Bangkok, both on the Chao Phraya River.

When King Rama I of the present Chakri Dynasty decided to relocate his capital from Dhonburi to Bangkok in 1782, one of his goals was to recreate the splendors of Ayutthaya. Outwardly, it was a traditional Thai capital, with traditional values. The king was still known as Chao Jivit, the Lord of Life. He was surrounded by arcane ritual and held absolute power over every aspect of his kingdom, from social matters to national defense.

Yet behind that facade, something new was stirring–or, perhaps more accurately, something as old as Sukhothai. King Ramkhamhaeng, the greatest of the rulers of the first capital, had established the concept of a benevolent, paternalistic monarchy, mindful of the needs of his people and accessible to them. This concept had not always been maintained in Ayutthaya, where rulers became increasingly aloof and even god-like, but early Bangkok saw a return to the ideal, along with deeply-rooted Buddhist beliefs. The king once more became a recognizable human being, explaining and justifying the various proclamations that issued from his glittering palace on the river.

By the time of Rama I's death, in 1809, stability had returned to the kingdom; his successors further defined the role of monarchy in Thai life, shrewdly adapting it to a world that was

Left: A foreigner of the 17th century, depicted in a gold-and-black lacquer painting.
Right: A map of Ayutthaya, a late 17th-century European drawing of a court mandarin, a detail from a temple mural showing foreigners, and a view of the royal barges at Ayutthaya.

changing with bewildering speed as neighbor after neighbor fell under European colonial rule. Bangkok, too, began to prosper, spurred by increased trade that attracted a growing number of Chinese immigrants. While most Thais preferred traditional occupations like farming and government service, the Chinese concentrated on commerce and were largely responsible for the city's remarkable growth.

To the average Westerner today, perhaps the best known of the early Chakri kings was Rama IV, or King Mongkut. Before coming to the throne in 1851, he spent 27 years in the Buddhist priesthood, a unique experience for a Thai ruler which in turn gave him unique insights into ordinary people's lives. He had travelled extensively, met foreign missionaries, learned English and French, and developed a keen interest in modern science; more than his predecessors, he recognized the danger of isolation, and through a series of wide-ranging reforms and treaties with foreign powers, he set his kingdom on a modern course.

King Chulalongkorn (Rama V) was a more than worthy successor. He reigned for 42 years and changed almost every aspect of Thai life, from government organization to fashions in dress and architecture. Pressure from England and France led to the loss of Thai territory in the far south and in Indo-China, but due to shrewd diplomacy it retained its treasured independence.

Left, top: The Chao Phraya River in the 1890s.
Left, bottom: An elephant roundup staged in the old kraal near Ayutthaya, late 19th century.
Opposite: Turn-of-the-century view of Bangkok's Golden Mount, once the highest elevation in the city, overlooking a busy canal.
Overleaf: Khmer-style *prangs* in the old capital of Ayutthaya, once a city of more than a million people.

Soon after King Chulalongkorn's death in 1910, the winds of change grew fiercer and more unpredictable. Because of its paternalistic nature, Thailand's absolute system survived longer than most; but it, too, ultimately succumbed to the demand for popular government. During the reign of King Prajadhipok (Rama VII), on 24 June 1932, a small group of officials, most of them foreign-educated, staged a *coup d'etat* in Bangkok and demanded a constitution. Already working along such lines, the king agreed, and so Thailand's ancient system, intact since Sukhothai, came to an end.

Disillusioned by the undemocratic regime that replaced him, King Prajadhipok abdicated in 1934. His successor was Prince Ananda Mahidol, a grandson of King Chulalongkorn and then a 10-year-old student in Switzerland. Except for a brief visit in 1938, the new king did not return to his homeland until the Pacific War ended, and tragedy ensued shortly afterward; on 9 June 1946, he died in the Grand Palace.

Thus his younger brother, the present monarch, came to the throne as King Bhumibol Aduljadej. The official coronation service took place in 1950, and at the same time the king married a beautiful young princess who became Queen Sirikit.

They have made rural development the hallmark of their reign, initiating programs that have ranged from new crops and methods of agriculture to water resources and the revival of traditional crafts. In the process, the king has become not only the best known of all the Chakri rulers but also the most beloved, a moral force that has held the country together in more than one period of political and economic unrest.

"This land of Sukhothai is thriving. There are fish in the water and rice in the fields. The lord of the realm does not levy toll on his subjects. They are free to lead their cattle or ride their horses and to engage in trade, whoever wants to trade in elephants, does so, whoever wants to trade in horses, does so, whoever wants to trade in silver or gold, does so."

— Stone inscription ascribed to King Ramkhamhaeng the Great, 1292

LAND & PEOPLE

"One morning early, we crossed the bar, and while the sun was rising splendidly over the flat spaces of land we steamed up the innumerable bends, passed under the shadow of the great gilt pagoda, and reached the outskirts of the town.

"There it was, spread largely on both banks, the Oriental capital which has yet suffered no white conqueror; an expanse of brown houses of bamboo, of mats, of leaves, of a vegetable-matter style of architecture, sprung out of the brown soil on the banks of the muddy river."

Thus, in 1888, Joseph Conrad described his first impressions of Thailand, or Siam as he and the rest of the world knew it then. The average visitor today gets a very different introduction. Certainly it is far less romantic: there may be a brief glimpse of chequered rice fields far below, perhaps the flash of a temple spire if the light is right, then suddenly the mundane buildings of modern metropolitan Bangkok and the air-conditioned anonymity of an international airport, all within a brief space of time. The land itself, some 513,115 square kilometers of highly varied topography, as well as its diverse people, remain to be discovered. And what a discovery that is!

Begin with the north, a logical place since this is probably where the Thais themselves first entered their future homeland. Here, the borders of present-day Burma and Laos meet those of Thailand in a panorama of rolling mountains. Teak and other hardwood trees are indigenous to the region and have provided basic building materials for centuries. In the cool, clear air–temperatures can drop to nearly freezing in the winter months–exotic plants flourish well: nearly a thousand species of wild orchids, festooning the trees like rare jewels when they bloom in the hot season, and secret fields of opium poppy grown by tribal groups who have migrated into that area newspaper readers know as the Golden Triangle.

Elephants, too, roam the forest, once in numerous wild herds. Now nearly all have been domesticated, originally for work in the logging camps and more recently to carry tourists on adventurous rides through the jungle. So-called "white elephants"–actually albinos–have traditionally been regarded as emblems of royalty and divinity and any that turn up are, by law, the property of the king and the object of great reverence.

Important rivers rise in the northern mountains, snaking southward through broad valleys and eventually linking to form the great Chao Phraya. Early settlements were founded in these valleys or on the great Mekong, which flows along the Laotian

Previous page: Water buffalo in a northern valley near Chiang Mai.
Left: A rural floating market, where all kinds of goods are sold by vendor boats.
Right: A typical Thai town street, culminating in a Buddhist monument. This one is in Nakhon Pathom in central Thailand; it was originally built by Mons and later expanded by Thais.

Left: Crops in a fertile river valley, one of countless similar ones throughout Thailand.
Right, top: Rice planting in the Central Plains, the country's most productive region.
Right, bottom: A traditional Thai house of the Central Plains type.
Overleaf: Vendor boats at a floating market, offering fruit, vegetables and spices.

border, among them Chiang Saen, Chiang Rai, Nan, Chiang Mai, and Lampang, all notable centers of power at one time or another. Even after more significant Thai states rose in the south, these northern principalities retained a remarkable degree of autonomy due to the difficulties of communication imposed by the rugged terrain. A railway line linking Bangkok and Chiang Mai was only opened in the late 1920s, and as recently as the 1960s tranquil little Mae Hong Son, nestling in the hills near Burma, was considered sufficiently remote to serve as a place of temporary exile for government officials in disgrace.

Though the river valleys of the north are fertile, supporting verdant fields of rice and fruit orchards, they were not really suitable for the development of a large-scale kingdom. In search of more space, the Thais, like other groups before them, were steadily drawn further into the great Chao Phraya river basin that lay just beyond the final chain of foothills like a fabled promised land.

Protected by mountains to the north and west and by the lofty Khorat Plateau to the east, the Central Plains region was part of the Gulf of Thailand millions of years ago. The rich soil of today was created by the steady accumulation of silt carried down every monsoon season by the highland rivers, at such a rate that the gulf shore continues to move southward by an estimated 5 meters a year. Dense forests covered the plains in prehistoric times. Today they are covered with a vast jigsaw puzzle of fields planted with rice and other crops, studded here and there with hamlets of simple houses, like islands in a sea of green. Down the middle, in great loops, winds the Chao Phraya.

Though only 365 kilometers in length it is of huge importance since it provides steady supplies of both water and rich topsoil.

The remains of the Thai past are scattered throughout this region, along with those of earlier settlers like the Khmers and the Mons. Sukhothai, the first truly independent Thai capital, lies in the northernmost part; then further down Lopburi, which was inhabited by all three groups; and then Ayutthaya, the greatest of all, from which the kingdom was ruled for four centuries. All these and other lesser cities drew their sustenance from the dependable fields, as would Bangkok, located not far from where the Chao Phraya emptied into the Gulf of Thailand.

Like Ayutthaya, early Bangkok was a riverine city–both were originally sited on artificial islands created by digging strategic canals–and drew its life from the Chao Phraya. Endless processions of teakwood barges brought–still bring, for that matter–essential foodstuffs from the countryside to the north; and from the Gulf other vessels like the one that carried Conrad brought different kinds of prosperity from another world beyond. Only after the Second World War did the river cease to be a major factor in the capital's existence, though it continues to serve as a vital artery for the Central Plains as a whole.

Previous page: A crowded scene at a market near Bangkok, where everything from fresh ingredients to a fast meal is available.
Left, top: A fishing boat getting ready to set sail from one of the countless ports of the south.
Left, bottom: Karon, one of the dozen or so scenic, white sand beaches along Phuket's coastline.
Opposite: An island offshore from Krabi. The Andaman Sea is dotted with hundreds of such islands; relatively few have been developed, but there are some hotels and guesthouses for that secret holiday of a lifetime.

The northeast, or Isan as it is called by Thais, is a very different story. Beginning at the Khorat Plateau, a tableland that occupies a third of Thailand's total area, and extending to the Mekong, it was once forested and apparently fertile. Drastic changes followed, however, perhaps due to destructive agricultural practices, perhaps to major climatic changes. In any event, the northeast became the country's chronic problem area, plagued by both droughts and floods.

Some idea of what the northeast may once have been like can be had at Khao Yai, at the beginning of the plateau only 206 kilometers from Bangkok. Established as a national park in 1959, this is a cool area of wooded hills and grassy valleys that supports a large number of protected wild animals, among them deer, monkeys, elephants and even an occasional tiger. There are streams wandering through the forest, picturesque waterfalls and, in the distance, lofty mountains.

Elsewhere, though, except for some rich land along the Mekong, most of the northeast has sandy soil that yields poor crops and a rainy season more irregular than the rest of the country. Its people, many of them ethnic Lao and Khmer, often abandon the farms and try their luck in cities like Bangkok, where they form the majority of the lower-level work forces.

In recent years, the region has attracted increasing government interest, and there are signs of a brighter economic future. New highways have been built and large reservoirs are relieving the age-old water problems; the introduction of new crops and farming methods is helping, too, as is the revival of traditional handicrafts like silk-weaving and pottery.

One of the country's most rapidly developing areas lies along the east coast of the Gulf, stretching from the Chao Phraya estuary to Trat Province on the Cambodian border. Long hampered by lack of good roads, this sector has now been opened and because of its proximity to the capital has become an important center for both industry and tourism. Pattaya, once a little-known fishing village, has become an internationally known seaside resort with scores of luxury hotels stretching along the long beach.

Sattahip, further down the coast, is the main Thai naval base and also an important deep-sea port for commercial cargoes. Chanthaburi, the last province before Trat, is home to luxuriant plantations of coconuts, durians, rambutans and pepper, as

Opposite: View of the valley at Mae Hong Son, a remote Thai province near the Burmese border.
Below: A woman crosses a bridge in a characteristic view of rural Thailand.

well as gem mines from which the famous Thai rubies and sapphires are extracted.

Southern Thailand is a long peninsula, bordered by the Gulf of Thailand on one side and the Indian Ocean on the other. It consists of 14 provinces and reaches like a probing elephant's trunk down to Malaysia. In many ways the south is a different world from the rest of Thailand, with its own centers of culture that developed independently of those in the north. Nakhon Sri Thammarat, for example, was already a thriving capital when Sukhothai was established in the 13th century, while Phuket, on the Indian Ocean, was known as Junkceylon to ancient mariners who came to trade at its ports. In the southernmost provinces, the dome of a mosque is as common as the spire of a Buddhist temple, due to a sizeable Muslim population that is often of Malay extraction.

Moreover, the region has natural resources of its own that have brought a prosperity rivalled only by that of the Central Plains. Rubber trees thrive in its damp climate, to such an extent that Thailand is one of the world's largest producers of natural rubber. Tin has for centuries been the source of Phuket's wealth and remains today one of the country's important exports, though it is now obtained by offshore dredges. Steep limestone cliffs and caves are favored havens for the tiny swifts whose nests are a prized delicacy in Chinese restaurants located many thousands of miles away.

Left: An Akha village, nestled in the high mountains of the far north; half a dozen hill tribes live in such settlements along Thailand's borders.

Above: A sampling of the various tribes of the north. In the top row, on the left is a Yao (Mien), in the middle a Karen, and on the right a Shan boy. In the bottom row, on the left is an Akha, in the middle a Long-Neck woman from a Paduang village, and on the right a Lisu.

The scenic beauty of the south is legendary. Along its center rises a chain of jungle-covered mountains, extending all the way into Malaysia. In some places, prehistoric cataclysms caused the sea to rush into low-lying coastal areas and create bays out of which limestone peaks emerge dramatically. The best known of these is Phangnga, near Phuket, where literally hundreds of outcroppings rise sheer from the water, many with fantastic stalagtite-hung caves and others with hidden crescents of pure white-sand beach.

Sun-drenched seashores and humid jungle, cities both ancient and resoundingly modern, miles of rice fields stretching to distant horizons and mist-enshrouded mountain peaks: these are the backgrounds against which the drama of Thailand's history has been enacted and which continue to shape the developments of today.

Left, top: Members of the Lahu (Mushur) hill tribe in traditional dress.
Left, bottom: Elephants at work; thousands of the animals were once employed in the teak forests of the north.
Opposite: A gathering of Lisu tribal people; their costumes and traditions have remained unchanged for centuries.

"The precepts which the religion of the Siamese prescribes for moral conduct are in conformity with the natural law which God has granted the souls of men for the conduct of their actions. These precepts can be reduced to two which subsume all the others: to avoid evil and practise good deeds. As for the observation of the first, the Siamese detest injustice, and are neither malicious, nor cruel, nor deceitful, and for the second they are very much inclined to observe it, displaying charity to everyone, especially to strangers, passers-by, animals and the dead."

— Jacques de Bourges, Jesuit missionary, 1663

RELIGION

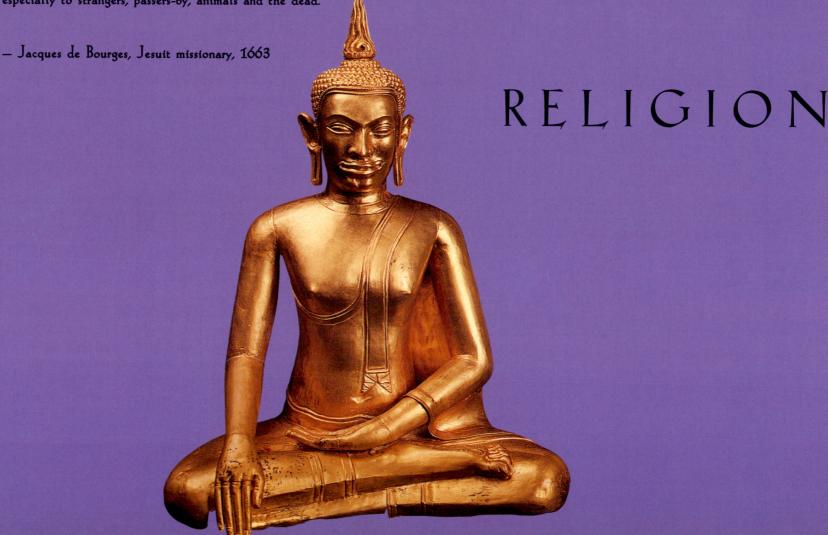

The festive procession moves along a country road to the infectious beat of long drums and cymbals, led by a group of dancers, all in their best clothes. At the center of the group rises a saffron-colored umbrella. Beneath it, borne on the shoulders of several friends, a young man, holding a candle, a flower and incense sticks in his clasped hands tries to maintain a dignified posture.

Early that morning–or perhaps the evening before–the young man's head and eyebrows were shaved, and he exchanged his ordinary clothes for white robes. Now, accompanied by family, friends and probably a handful of strangers attracted by the music, he is on his way to the village monastery for one of the basic rituals of Thai life.

Though few of the participants are aware of it, ancient symbolism pervades nearly every aspect of this familiar undertaking. The loss of his hair represents the willing sacrifice of his individuality, while the white vestments connote purity. The saffron umbrella is a reminder of the royal accoutrements that Prince Siddharta Guatama renounced in order to attain the supreme goal of Buddhahood. When he reaches the monastery, the young man will walk around the main building three times to evoke the Triple Gem: Buddha, Dhamma and Sangha (Teacher, Teaching and Taught). And the offerings he carries symbolize the transitory nature of life (the candle), the impermanence of beauty (the flower), and the fragrance of a pure life (the incense sticks).

Once inside the temple, the young man undergoes a sort of catechism conducted by senior priests and swears to uphold the ten major precepts of novice monkhood. He then discards his white robes for saffron ones and becomes for a time–usually for a few weeks or months, sometimes for life–one of the Buddha's disciples.

Buddhism came to Thailand in the 3rd century BC, when missionaries of the Theravada sect were sent by the Indian Emperor Asoka. They preached the faith in the semi-legendary kingdom of Suvannabhumi, near the present-day provincial capital of Nakhon Pathom, and it proved so popular that the Mons who arrived later adopted it as their state religion, as did the independent Thai kingdom of Sukhothai.

Today, over 90 percent of the Thai people are Theravada Buddhists and there are some 27,000 *wats* or monasteries, scattered about the country, distinguished by their multi-tiered roofs and elaborate decorations. In large urban centers like Bangkok, the effect of the faith on daily life may be difficult for outsiders to perceive, but Buddhist values are deeply embedded, absorbed from family teachings, the educational system and countless other social influences. They lie behind such familiar expressions as *mai pen rai* ("never mind, it doesn't matter"), which reflects an acceptance of misfortunes beyond one's control and the Thai ideal of a "cool heart", avoiding extremes of emotion whenever possible.

In the countryside, where most Thais live, the active role of Buddhism is far more apparent. Village *wats* generally serve as community centers, and senior monks may be called upon to advise and arbitrate in local disputes. Until he has served a

Previous page: Buddhist monks, a familiar sight in every Thai settlement.
Opposite: Wat Doi Suthep, on a hill overlooking Chiang Mai, one of the most famous northern temples.
Right: Monks receiving food from laymen, a daily morning ritual all over Thailand and one of the basic ways for Buddhists to earn merit for their future existences.

period as a monk, a young man is regarded as *khon dip*, an "unripe person," and few local girls would consider marrying him. In more remote areas, the government school may use a *wat* building for classes, and nearly all festivals, Buddhists and otherwise, are held in the *wat* compound.

Perhaps the most obvious Buddhist activities are those that involve making merit in order to improve one's present existence as well as those that lie in the unknown future. Every morning, in both cities and countryside, Buddhist monks can be seen accepting food from laymen, a rite as common today as in the distant past. No "begging" is involved in the transaction, as so many Western observers mistakenly assume; if anyone is grateful, it is the layman rather than the monk, for he is the one who truly benefits from the pious act.

The desire to make merit was the motivation behind the construction of the great temples of Thailand, from Sukhothai to Bangkok, as well as for their adornment and frequent refurbishing. Wealthy members of the community donate funds for such purposes, and the less affluent offer their physical labors. Merit is also made by building hospitals and schools, giving alms to beggars, or participating in a charitable activity.

In tolerant Thailand, however, where selective assimilation has been a notable trait since ancient times, Buddhism is not the only belief that makes itself apparent. Other spiritual forces are

Opposite: The Emerald Buddha, the most revered of all Thailand's images, enshrined at Bangkok's Wat Phra Keo in the Grand Palace Compound.
Right, top and bottom: Scenes from an ordination ceremony, an important ritual in Thai life; every young man is expected to enter the monkhood for a time at some point.

also at work, often so intricately interwined that it is difficult to separate them into convenient categories.

Brahmin rituals, for example, came to Thailand in the early Ayutthaya period and soon became an integral part of many ceremonies, especially those involving royalty. Brahmin priests continue to play an important role in many rituals, among them the Plowing Ceremony held annually outside the Grand Palace in April to inaugurate the rice planting season.

Much older beliefs are also strong. In every village, and most cities as well, there is a small structure that is the object of considerable attention from the inhabitants. Generally this is a small house raised on a post, perhaps a basic wooden affair that resembles a model of a traditional Thai dwelling, perhaps a fancy cement creation in bright colors with elaborate decorations. In either case, it is neatly tended and kept supplied with regular offerings.

This is the communal spirit house, home of the invisible guardians of the village. Spirits, or *phis* as they are known in Thai, are older than Buddhism, as old, indeed, as man, and belief in them answers deeply rooted needs left unsatisfied by philosophical faiths. From the earliest times there have been *phis* of the earth, of the air, of the water, of certain trees; others, too, that watch over communities, homes, even individual rooms. If angered, these unseen beings can cause all sorts of disasters, from crop failure to infertility. Properly placated, however–with

Left: A priest invoking spirits of the city at the Wieng Lakhon ceremony in Lampang; offerings of various kinds are made at the shrine.
Opposite: Assorted spirit houses and offerings; animist and other beliefs have coexisted with Buddhism for centuries in Thailand.

burning incense, fragrant flowers, sometimes something special like fireworks or dancers—they will refrain from such mischief and bring peace and prosperity.

Such ancient beliefs were not displaced by Buddhism but either continued to coexist alongside the new faith or were actually absorbed by it. It is not uncommon to find monks enlisted to find a suitable spot for a spirit house or to come across such a dwelling within the precincts of a *wat*.

Especially in urban areas, Chinese beliefs are also much in evidence. Every city has its brightly-decorated Chinese temple, and most shops have a red-and-gilt shrine before which daily offerings are made; many merchants, too, display a small figure of a female deity known as Nang Kwok, whose arm is raised in a beckoning gesture to lure customers to the premises. During eclipses, local Chinese take to the streets beating drums to avert the end of the world, and Chinese New Year, though not officially recognized, is nevertheless a time of ceremonies, festivities and an unnatural quiet in normally bustling business districts.

Buddhism in its purest form disdains belief in the supernatural. Nevertheless, such concepts clearly fulfil fundamental needs, and in Thailand, as elsewhere, they continued to figure prominently in daily life, adding to its color and variety.

Left: Offerings are carried to a temple on an elephant in a northern merit-making ceremony.
Opposite: The Songkran festival in Lampang, celebrating the old Thai New Year with processions and rituals.

Above: Assorted offerings made at shrines, temples and ceremonies; both flowers and objects are believed to appeal to certain spirits.
Opposite: A cave temple at Chiang Dao, inspired by some of the earliest Buddhist temples of India.

 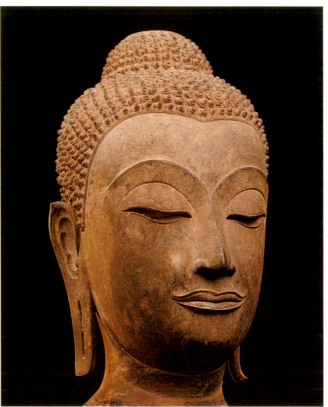

Above: Heads of the Buddha; the one on the left is Ayutthaya style while the one on the right came from Lopburi.
Opposite: Detail from a mural painting depicting the life of the Buddha; here the Buddha is seen ascending a stair to heaven, surrounded by divinities.
Overleaf: Wat Phra Singh in Chiang Mai. Founded in 1345, when Chiang Mai was the capital of the northern Lanna Thai kingdom, this famous temple has been restored many times; the structure on the left is in Lanna style.

"The King comes out of the city, accompanied by the whole of the nobility, in barges richly gilded and covered with ornaments, with great display and noise of musical instruments. They proclaim the King is about to order the waters to disperse, and this is the great festival of the year. A mast is raised in the middle of the stream, adorned with silken flags, and a prize suspended for the best rower. All the contending boats put themselves in trim, and at a given signal start, with such cries, and shouting, and tumults, as if the world was being destroyed.... "

— Diogo Do Couto, Portuguese adventurer (1543)

FESTIVALS

A famous stone inscription, attributed to King Ramkhamhaeng of Sukhothai, describes a merit-making procession to a forest monastery outside the capital. "When they are ready to return to the city," it says, "they walk together, forming a line all the way to the parade-ground. They join together in striking up the sound of musical instruments, chanting and singing. Whoever wants to make merry, does so; whoever wants to laugh, does so. As this city of Sukhothai has four very big gates, and as the people always crowd together to come in and watch the lighting of candles and setting off of fireworks, the city is noisy as if it was bursting."

Music and merrymaking, laughter and songs, crowds of people and exploding fireworks–seven centuries later, this is still an accurate description of many of the traditional festivals scattered throughout the Thai year. Though some may be essentially serious, they usually have a lighter side as well, a generous infusion of what the Thais call *sanuk*, or fun.

Take, for instance, the northeastern *bun bang fai*, or skyrocket festival. This incorporates Brahmanical, Buddhist and animist elements and is basically concerned with bringing abundant rain to that often drought-stricken part of Thailand. At the same time, it provides an opportunity for a good deal of high-spirited behavior that is normally suppressed within the rather conservative village culture.

The same is true of Songkran, which marks the beginning of the old Thai new year. The ceremonial part of Songkran consists of bringing offerings to local monasteries and annointing both the abbot and the principal Buddha images with lustral water; homes are also given a thorough cleaning, and elder members of the family are sprinkled with water by the younger as a sign of respect.

Thereafter, the spirit of *sanuk* takes over. Instead of ritual water-sprinkling, whole buckets are thrown, with any passer-by being fair game. No one minds, though–the weather is hot enough to make a cool bath welcome and it is, after all, Songkran.

For beauty, no Thai festival can really compare with Loy Krathong, held on the full-moon night of the 11th lunar month. This pays homage to the water spirits. Thai legend says it originated in Sukhothai when a lady of the court, seeking to please her royal master, deftly folded banana leaves in the shape of a lotus blossom, which she then adorned with flowers, incense sticks and a lighted candle. The innovation so pleased the king that Loy Krathong became an annual event, celebrated today by setting thousands of little boats adrift on rivers and canals all over the country.

Some festivals are peculiar to a particular province or even a town. Phuket, for example, has a 10-day Vegetarian Festival. Essentially a Chinese celebration, this has turned into an all-island event with parades, music and dancing; many of the participants go into trances and peform quite spectacular feats of self-mortification such as walking on red-hot coals and piercing their bodies with spikes. Chiang Mai has a Flower Festival, with awards for the best blossom-bedecked float, and Lampang has a

Previous page: The Loy Krathong festival at Sukhothai, where according to legend the magic ritual originated more than seven centuries ago.
Left, top: Children place a lighted candle, incense sticks, and a coin for luck in each lotus-shaped *krathong* before setting them adrift.
Left, bottom: Traditional Thai dancing and pretty girls, always part of the Loy Krathong celebration.
Opposite: Ancient Sukhothai returns to life each year when the Loy Krathong festival is staged in its ponds and moats.

Left: The Royal Barge Procession, now held only on special occasions such as the Golden Jubilee, is one of the most magnificent Thai spectacles. Dozens of incredibly carved and gilded barges, some dating from early Bangkok, carry the King in state along the Chao Phraya River, while some 2,000 oarsmen in traditional costumes chant rythmically. The largest of the vessels, the Supphanahongsa, is over 50 meters long, adorned with a mythical, swan-like bird at its prow. The purpose of the procession is to bring alms to riverside temples, particularly Wat Arun, the Temple of Dawn, on the Thonburi side.

Opposite, top: Traditional costumes worn by oarsmen who propel the huge barges.

Opposite, bottom: One of the ornate barges, most of which are hewn from a single teak log.

Garlic Festival, complete with the crowning of a local beauty selected as Miss Garlic.

Temple murals with scenes of life in early Bangkok often show a rapt crowd gathered before theatrical performances. The rarest of these today, at least in its full unabbreviated glory, is the *khon*, or masked dance drama. The *khon* plot is derived from the Ramakien, the Thai version of the Indian Ramayana, an epic account of the triumph of good over evil. Many of the characters wear magnificent papier-maché masks, and the story is told through a vocabulary of stylized postures and gestures, expressing not only action but also thought and feeling.

Khon was originally limited to the royal court but eventually moved outside the palace walls in a form called *lakhon*, which draws its stories from other traditional sources but with similar costumes and gestures. A subdivision, *lakhon chatri*, is performed by women and groups can often be seen dancing at various shrines, hired by grateful supplicants whose wishes have been granted by the resident spirit.

Also rare today is *nang yai*, the shadow-play, the earliest Thai dance-drama which was probably introduced from Indonesia. Intricately shaped figures made of cowhide, depicting characters from the Ramakien, are held behind a lighted screen and move to the accompaniment of music and choral singing. In a more popular version called *nang talung*, still to be seen in the far south, the figures are smaller and often have one moveable part such as a chin or arm; concealed along with the manipulators are singers and comedians whose witty contributions probably account for the continuing life of the form.

Certain rituals are part of everyday life. Some traditional families still stage a top-knot cutting ceremony to celebrate a child's coming of age, usually presided over by a Brahmin priest, and, in most, it is a joyous occasion when a son is ordained as a Buddhist monk for a period. Old costumes are customarily worn at Thai weddings, the celebration of a 60th birthday (that is, completion of the fifth 12-year cycle) is a major event, and cremation rites at a temple go on for days or even months depending on the deceased's importance and rank. In addition, of course, there are such customs as making daily offerings to the resident spirit, giving food to monks, visiting various shrines, and ceremonies to honor revered teachers.

Many of the duties of Thailand's much-loved monarchy are ceremonial, and splendor as well as tradition is important in these. The magnificent Royal Barge Procession, when the king is rowed in state down the Chao Phraya River in a fleet of carved and gilded barges, is seldom seen nowadays, though it was staged for several important recent events such as the celebrations of the Chakri Dynasty's bicentennial in 1982, the king's 60th birthday in 1987 and the Royal Jubilee in 1996. Others, however, are regular events that take place throughout the year.

There is, for instance, the annual royal Plowing Ceremony, an ancient Brahmin ritual that goes back to Ayutthaya times and that was revived by the present king. Thousands of spectators come to Sanam Luang, the oval field across from the Grand Palace, to watch a symbolic rice-planting ritual and learn from various omens what the coming season will bring.

Opposite: A hilltribe boy at the Loy Krathong celebration in Chiang Mai.
Below: An imaginative Loy Krathong decoration displayed in a lake.
Right: Winner of a beauty contest, one of the popular features of most Thai festivals.

Three times a year, the king presides over the changing of the robes of the sacred Emerald Buddha, spiritual guardian of the kingdom: a golden, diamond-studded tunic for the hot season, a gilded robe flecked with blue stones for the rainy months, and one of enamel-coated solid gold, covering the image from head to toe, for the cool season.

As Head of the Armed Forces, he is the focus of the annual Trooping of the Colors, a grand display of brilliant uniforms held in the Royal Plaza near the equestrian statue of his grandfather, King Chulalongkorn. There are also countless other events transformed by the king's presence into memorable occasions: university graduation ceremonies when the proud graduates personally receive their degrees from his hands, the presentation of credentials by new foreign ambassadors, the casting of Buddha images at various temples, the sprinkling of lustral water at wedding celebrations and cremations of important citizens are but a few examples.

Royal or religious, solemn or full of *sanuk*–sometimes a combination of all these–festivals and ceremonies form an integral part of Thai life.

Far left: Colorful banners displayed outside the library of an old monastery in Chiang Mai during the New Year celebration.
Left: Homage is paid to the revered Phra Buddha Sihing image at Wat Phra Singh in Chiang Mai.
Right, top and bottom: Large crowds turn out for Songkran, celebrating the old Thai New Year, during which Buddha images are paraded through the streets and water is thrown with cheerful abandon.

"It was the custom of many of the wealthy families to maintain craftsmen in their own houses. Some were employed as gold and silver smiths, some as jewellers, others were painters and woodcarvers, or workers in lacquer or in mother-of-pearl... the artists belonged to the household, they took pride in their work, they vied with each other in performance, and their children when they grew up entered the occupation and learnt it from their parents."

— Malcolm Smith, *A Physician at the Court of Siam* (1957)

ARTS & CRAFTS

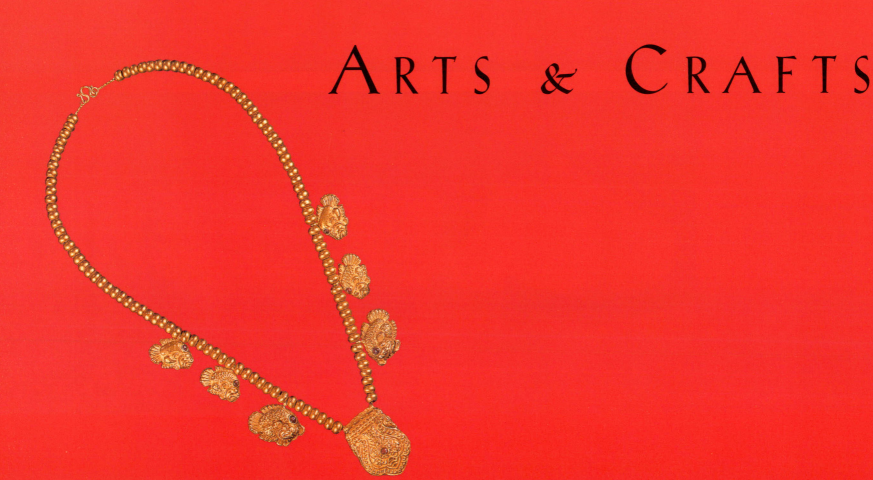

Thailand has a rich tradition of crafts, handed down over generations since the earliest days of the kingdom. Some, like the lustrous silks of the northeast, have become internationally renowned, while others, like celadon stoneware and finely wrought nielloware bowls, occasionally rise to the lofty heights of fine art. And countless more continue to be made and serve practical needs in the obscurity of rural villages, little known to the sophisticated world outside.

Baskets, for example, are deftly woven from thin strips of bamboo and other native plants, and special ones have evolved for almost every purpose. There are a number of different kinds of traps to catch fish and containers to protect them on the journey home. The multi-purpose *grajad* is used for carrying rice and other produce, and another kind of basket is especially made to store glutinous rice, the staple food of the north and northeast. Still others are made for winnowing rice, for measuring coconuts, for rearing silkworms and for storing clothes–in fact, for just about every conceivable need that might arise in the course of everyday rural existence.

Numerous commonplace items are given an elegance of line or design that makes them more than merely functional. Coconut scrapers, for instance, often take the form of beautifully carved animals–rabbits, pigs, cats and elephants–with a scraping device extending from the mouth; the worker can thus use the animal as a convenient seat while husking the nuts. Simple pottery is made throughout the country, each region having certain distinctive designs of its own, while supple mats, made by plaiting reeds or strips of palm leaf, often have intricate colored designs and are used on the floors of almost every rural house.

One highly perishable category of crafts consists of floral decorations used in countless ceremonies. These are not "arrangements" in the Western sense of the term; the Thai aim, instead, is to turn flowers into objects of beauty that have no counterpart in nature but that proudly proclaim the artistic skills of man.

Among the traditional styles, the most commonly seen are *malai*, or garlands. These play a prominent part in Thai social and religious life. Fragrant jasmine buds are the basis for most of these, but numerous other flowers may be used. *Malai* range from reasonably simple creations, like those sold on street corners and outside every shrine, to large and complex wreaths, requiring hours of work and costing hundreds of baht. Another kind is *jad paan*, or bowl arrangements, in which the flowers are embedded in a mound of damp clay or sawdust and then placed in a low, footed bowl; the results resemble exquisite, multi-colored pieces of porcelain.

Banana leaves can also be turned by skillful hands into many lovely objects. One group, known as *bai sri*, are complicated creations consisting of folded leaves, flowers and sometimes food. These are offered to a spirit house or displayed during a number of ceremonies. A classic *bai sri* is the little lotus-shaped float called the *krathong*, which is set adrift with lighted candles as part of the Loy Krathong festival.

Undoubtedly, the greatest concentration of Thai handicrafts today is found in the north, particularly in and around Chiang Mai. The various artisans used to live outside the old city walls, each group in a special village specializing in a particular craft. Over the years, these communities became absorbed into the growing city and so lost their identity; but even today, their

Previous page: Silver and gold containers and footed trays, crafted for royalty.
Opposite: Details of a panel decorated with lacquer paintings, in late 18th-century Ayutthaya style; the art was perfected in Ayutthaya and also continued in the early Bangkok period to adorn doors, windows and manuscript cabinets.
Below: A craftsman demonstrating the lacquer-ware technique of *lai rod nam* or "design from washing", whereby gold leaf is revealed on a stark black lacquered background.

ancestors often continue to live in the same areas and to produce the same sorts of objects.

No northern ritual, now or in the distant past, would be complete without a silver bowl, usually one adorned with elaborate *repoussé* decorations made by patiently tapping out the design on sheets of silver on a wooden mould. Lacquerware is another classic Chiang Mai craft, produced by giving a base of woven bamboo up to 15 coats of gummy resin to create a shiny surface; since each coat can take as long as two weeks to dry in damp weather, a simple bowl may take several months to make. Many Thai lacquer objects are further embellished–and sometimes elevated to the status of high art–by a process called *lai rod nam*, in which they are adorned with bright gold decorations against the glossy black background.

Woodcarving is a justly famous northern art. Temples of the region are lavishly decorated with ornate pediments, cornices, lintels and roofends, and the skill is also evident in countless domestic items. Today, when a new restaurant in Bangkok or a hotel in distant Phuket requires high-quality carving, Chiang Mai artisans are frequently brought all the way down to execute the work on the spot.

In the village of Bor Sang, outside the provincial capital, nearly the entire population is engaged in the production of

Left: Classic Thai decorations at Wat Phra Keo, the Temple of the Emerald Buddha.
Opposite, left: Inlaid mother-of-pearl decorations.
Opposite, right top: Contemporary Bencharong porcelain bowls, embellished with a garland of jasmine flowers.
Opposite, right bottom: Finely-wrought gold containers in traditional styles.

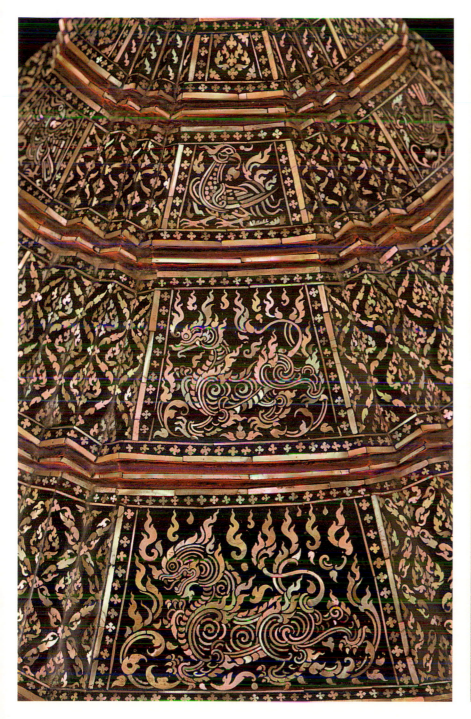

elegant parasols. Locally made paper is stretched over a bamboo frame and then strikingly decorated with paintings of flowers, dragons, scenic views and other patterns.

The latest of northern handicrafts, at least as far as popularity in the outside world is concerned, are those made by tribal people living along the borders of Burma and Laos. Nearly all are gifted silversmiths, for the very practical reason that heavy jewellry is an easy way to carry their wealth on their nomadic wanderings. Fine embroidery is also a traditional hill-tribe art, with the Hmong and Yao people being particularly skilled at creating bold, geometric designs in cotton.

On the international market, certainly the best-known Thai product is silk, the shimmering fabric now regarded as a standard luxury item by decorators and designers all over the world. The skill is an ancient one, already practised in the first Thai capital of Sukhothai and perhaps even earlier. Eventually, during the Bangkok period, the industry became largely concentrated in the northeast, where mulberry trees grow plentifully and silk-weaving served as a way of earning extra income between rice harvests.

Silk designs in the old days denoted rank, and it was part of every ceremonial costume. In the early years of the present century, however, production declined because of changing fashions and a flood of cheaper, mass-produced textiles from abroad. It was a remarkable American named Jim Thompson

Left: A woodcarver at work in Chiang Mai; such products created by northern artisans not only adorn temples and houses but also many luxury hotels.

who revived the industry just after the Second World War. He persuaded weavers to start making longer lengths of the cloth, introduced color-fast chemical dyes and built up a thriving export industry. When Thai silk was used for the costumes in the popular musical "The King and I," it became an international sensation.

Despite all the changes, silk-making in Thailand remains basically a cottage industry, and the techniques of sericulture are more or less the same as they were centuries ago. Newly hatched silk-worms are carefully tended in large, shallow trays and regularly fed with tender mulberry leaves. After about 30 days, the worms abruptly stop eating and hold up their heads, a signal that they are ready to start spinning their cocoons. This takes another three days, after which the cocoons are either sold to factories or reeled by the family who raised the worms.

The line between handicraft and fine art becomes blurred in many traditional Thai products, especially those made for royal or religious use. Lacquer inlaid with intricate designs of mother-of-pearl shell resulted in magnificent works during the Ayutthaya and early Bangkok periods, when temple doors and windows, manuscript boxes and betel nut sets were splendidly decorated by the painstaking process the Thais call *krueng mook.*

Celadon has been produced in the country since the Sukhothai period, and certainly many of the ancient pieces rank high in the world of great Asian ceramics; after centuries of

Right: Detail from a carved and gilded temple decoration showing a Thai divinity standing on the back of an earth-eating ogre, surrounded by traditional motifs.

decline, the art was revived in Chiang Mai, using the same techniques that produced the classic specimens. Nielloware, or *krueng tom*, came from either China or Persia–scholars differ on the precise origin–but it became one of the major crafts of southern Thailand and is still produced there today. Using either silver or gold, artisans etch traditional designs which stand out against the sharp black, gleaming metal background of the completed object, be it a bowl, a tea pot or a royal throne.

Woodcarving, too, often achieves the level of fine art. Temple decorations and items such as seats made for senior priests to use while delivering sermons, and non-religious articles like classical Thai musical instruments are lovingly carved and crafted. The earliest musical instruments were fairly simple and often named after the sound they made–*chap*, *ching*, *khong* and *klong*, for instance–but in time they became far more complex. Among these were the xylophone-like *ranat ek* and *ranat thum*, as well as the three-stringed *so sam sai*, which produces tunes of haunting poignancy.

From simple baskets to a refined musical instrument or a piece of palace goldwork may seem a broad step indeed; all, however, derive from the same innate sense of delicate craftsmanship that is one of the indisputible glories of Thailand's diverse culture.

Left, top: Dyed thread is reeled, one of the steps in silk weaving.
Left, bottom: A craftswoman demonstrates the technique of knotting or binding the threads on an *ikat* textile loom. This produces an elaborate design in the weave, a characteristic of these woven textiles.
Opposite: Thais in traditional skirts and shoulder cloths for a ceremony, carrying handmade umbrellas.

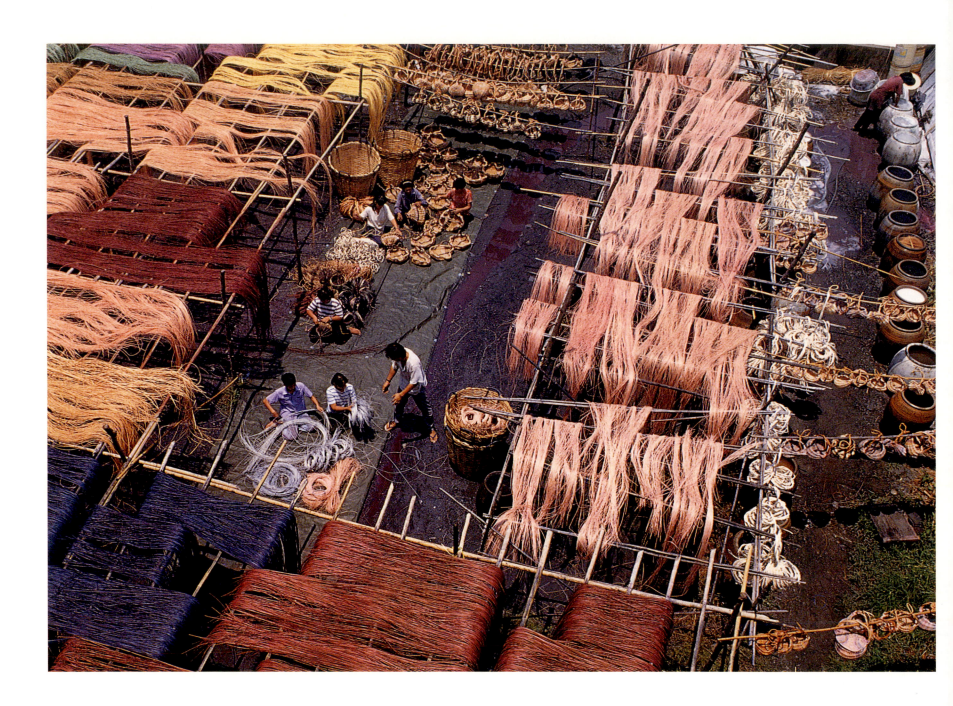

Above: Dyeing materials used to weave baskets, a craft found in almost every Thai household.

Above: Umbrellas, composed of handmade paper stretched over a bamboo frame; in Bor Sang, a village near Chiang Mai, all the inhabitants earn a living from this craft.

Above: Thailand is a paradise for shoppers! Some of the items available include (top left) a Bencharong tea set in Chinese style, (top right) contemporary hand-fired celadon pots, (bottom left) masks made for traditional dance-drama and (bottom right) silk cushion covers from the Jim Thompson range.

Above: (Top left) shows some of the delightful hand-woven baskets available, (top right) showcases photo-frames, boxes and bags in Jim Thompson silk, (bottom left) a selection of lacquerware receptacles and (bottom right) sparkling, gem-studded Thai jewellery.

Above: *Khon*, the classical dance-drama, draws its story from the Ramakien, the Thai version of the Indian Ramayana epic. Major characters wear papier-maché masks and convey emotions through stylized gestures.
Opposite: *Nang yai*, the shadow play, is thought to have come to Thailand from Indonesia; large figures made of cowhide are held behind a lighted screen and moved to the accompaniment of music and choral singing.
Overleaf: A unique set of miniature *hun lek* puppets; featuring extremely intricate costumes and masks, this type of puppet show is seen rarely. From a set at Bangkok's National Museum.

VISITING THAILAND

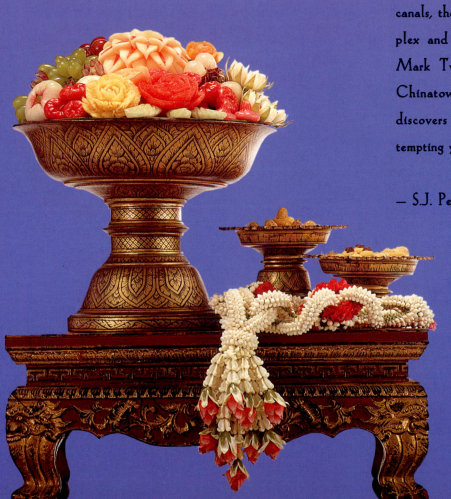

"From the very beginning I was charmed by Bangkok and I propose to be agressively syrupy about it in the most buckeye travelogue manner. I liked its polite, gentle, handsome people, its temples, flowers and canals, the relaxed and peaceful rhythm of life there... Its character is complex and inconsistent, it seems to combine the Hannibal, Missouri, of Mark Twain's boyhood with Beverly Hills, the Low Countries and Chinatown... The effect is indescribably pleasing, your eye constantly discovers new vistas, isolated little communities around every corner tempting you to explore them."

— S.J. Perelman, *Westward Ha!* (1948)

One of the joys of a visit to Thailand lies in discovering some of the assorted aspects that give the kingdom its particular style, making it different from any other travel destination. These may cover a wide range–for instance, a temple building that expresses exuberant joy as well as pious devotion, the sight of an elephant strolling along a jungle trail, a Thai meal in which each distinctive flavor comes as a revelation, perhaps only a shy smile glimpsed on the veranda of a traditional house.

Somerset Maugham, on a visit in 1923, was at first depressed by the outward aspect of Bangkok, which seemed to him composed of "dust and heat and noise and whiteness and more dust." Then he came across the city's numerous Buddhist temples and found enchantment: "They are unlike anything in the world, so that you are taken aback, and you cannot fit them into the scheme of the things you know. It makes you laugh with delight to think that anything so fantastic could exist on this somber earth."

The temples are still there, sparkling like gigantic, bejewelled wedding cakes in the sunlight across an expanse of emerald-green rice fields, hushed oases of quiet in the middle of noisy cities. So are their domestic equivalents, plain wooden structures with few

decorations yet with an elegant steepness of roof, a hint of fantasy in the curving ornaments at the tip of bargeboards that makes them distinctive. Thai houses can now be found outside rural settings, where for centuries they have served the practical needs of farmers; more affluent city people have come to see them as a reaffirmation of national identity and luxury resorts are using them imaginatively in exotic locations.

"Wherever we are and whatever we are doing, we like first and best to eat," a Thai writer has observed. As this suggests, eating ranks high on the Thai scale of pleasures, and whether simple or grand, a meal can provide extensive insight into the kingdom's character. Rice forms the centerpiece—fragrant and loose-grained in most parts of the country, glutinous in the north and northeast—and the other dishes are placed around it, to be eaten in whatever order the diner prefers and seasoned to individual taste with such condiments as fish sauce and chilli peppers. Usually there will be a soup of some kind, a curry, a steamed or fried dish, a salad, and one or more basic sauces; dessert may consist of a selection of the country's celebrated fruits—mango, durian, rambutan, mangosteen, to mention only a few—or one of several traditional sweets.

Previous page: A group of Thai-style buildings, here adapted for use in a popular health spa on the Gulf of Thailand.
Opposite: The drawing room of the Jim Thompson house, the most famous of all the Thai-style homes adapted to modern living.
Right, top and bottom: Houses in the traditional central style, less ornate than the kingdom's Buddhist temples but with a special elegance all their own.

Left: A decorative piece of northern woodcarving has been used as the headboard for a bed in this traditional Thai interior.

Opposite: Thai style at its most refined; old manuscript cabinets, tables, and silk cushions in the lofty teak living room of an old house.

Thai food comes in more varieties than an outsider might suspect from experiences in London and Los Angeles. Each region has its own specialties, from the spicy yams or salads of the northeast, to the Muslim-style curries of the far south, from the noodle-based street food of Bangkok to Burmese-inspired dishes of the north. Travelling around the country becomes a journey of culinary revelation, as constantly surprising as the ever-changing scenery.

Other discoveries, too, are unique to Thailand. In the hot season, for instance, after a steamy tour of the splendid Grand Palace, a visitor may find himself enthralled by a different sort of diversion in the large oval field known as Sanam Luang, just outside the palace walls. The blue sky is likely to be filled with kites, not just familiar, diamond-shaped ones but also enormous star-shaped creations measuring several meters across.

This is Thai kite fighting, actually an aerial battle of the sexes, in which dainty little "female" kites defend their territory against predatory raids by huge "males," each of which requires a team of up to 20 strong men to maneuver. As in life, the darting females prove an elusive prey and as often as not manage to bring their opponents crashing to the earth, cheered by spectactors enjoying the match from the comfort of reclining chairs.

Left: A dining area at one of the villas of the Amanpuri, a Phuket resort that uses traditional style in innovative ways; the triangular cushions are covered with Thai cotton.
Opposite, top left: A selection of Thai condiments.
Opposite, top right: A set of silver utensils used for betel nut.
Opposite, bottom left: A banana-leaf container for Thai sweets.
Opposite, bottom right: A Thai meal, presented in classic style.

Thai-style boxing is just as distinctive. Known abroad as "kick boxing," it is probably the kingdom's favorite traditional sport and has been since the Ayutthaya period. Bouts are accompanied by a three-piece orchestra, which sits to one side of the ring and keeps pace with the action, stimulating both fighters and spectators. Any part of the body except the head can be used as an offensive weapon, and any part, *including* the head, is a fair target. The foot is the most effective of all, usually swung in a wide arc at lightning speed, and the whole performance has a balletic grace that belies its deadly purpose.

Or perhaps the visitor will prefer something that is pure grace, without the violence, like *takraw*, a sport that involves keeping a hollow rattan ball aloft as long as possible by players who can use their feet, knees, elbows and head, but not their hands. Groups of young men set up a casual game of *takraw* almost anywhere during a break from work or school, and there are professional teams who perform truly dazzling stunts in the course of a match.

Discovery of Thailand's special appeal may come on a pristine beach that fulfills a host of escapist dreams, on a visit to one of the exotic hill tribes of the far north, over a memorable meal, even on a mundane street in Bangkok that seems to offer nothing and then suddenly reveals an unexpected wonder. Sooner or later, though, it comes to almost every visitor, and lingers in the memory forever after.

Left, top and bottom: Traditional buildings are often used today for entertaining, providing a distinctive background in both homes and restaurants.
Opposite: The reception pavilion at the Amanpuri in Phuket; many resorts have discovered the powerful appeal of classic Thai architecture.

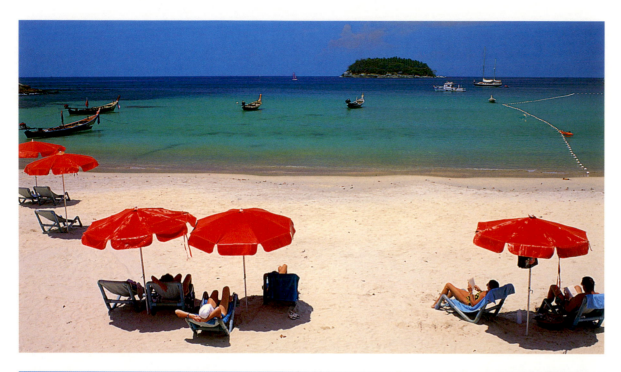

Left, top and bottom: Along both the Gulf of Thailand and the Andaman Sea, countless beautiful beaches offer year-round serenity.

Opposite: The swimming pool at the Chiva Som, a spa on the Gulf of Thailand at Hua Hin, where Thai-style buildings are used for modern health treatments.

Above: An offshore island in the Andaman Sea, surrounded by white-sand beaches and crystal-clear waters ideal for swimming and diving.

Above: A beach on Koh Phi Phi in the far south, one of the more recent islands to have been "discovered" by foreign travellers.

Selected Further Reading

Ancient Capitals of Thailand, Elizabeth Moore et al, Weatherhill, 1996

The Art of Southeast Asia: Cambodia, Vietnam, Thailand, Laos, Java, Bali, Philip S Rawson,
World of Art, 1990

The Arts of Thailand, Steve Van Beek, Periplus Editions, reprinted 1998

Bridge Over the River Kwai, Pierre Boulle, Amereon Ltd, 1988

The Colours of Thailand, Barbara Lloyd (photographer) Thames & Hudson, 1997

Descriptions of Old Siam, Michael Smithies (compiler), Oxford in Asia, 1996

The Food of Thailand: Authentic Recipes from the Golden Kingdom, Periplus World Cookbooks,
Periplus Editions, 1994

Gardening in Bangkok, Pimsai Amranand and William Warren, The Siam Society,
reprinted 1994

A Guide to the Khmer Temples in Thailand and Laos, Michael Freeman (photographer),
Weatherhill, 1998

Jim Thompson, The Undsolved Mystery, William Warren, Houghton Mifflin, reprinted 1998

Thai Garden Style, William Warren, Periplus Editions, 1996

Oriental Art, A Handbook of Styles and Forms, Jeannine Auboyer, Michel Beurdeley,
Jean Boisselier, Huguette Rousset and Chantel Massonaud, London, 1979

Traditional Festivals in Thailand, Ruth Gerson, Images of Asia, 1996